Dear Diary; I Don't Think That Word Means What I Think It Means

Dear Diary Style Files, Volume 5

Saoirse Temple

Published by Saoirse Temple, 2025.

While every precaution has been taken in the preparation of this book, the publisher assumes no responsibility for errors or omissions, or for damages resulting from the use of the information contained herein.

DEAR DIARY; I DON'T THINK THAT WORD MEANS WHAT I THINK IT MEANS

First edition. September 15, 2025.

Copyright © 2025 Saoirse Temple.

ISBN: 978-1069750532

Written by Saoirse Temple.

Table of Contents

Before We Begin: A Word About Words 1
Entry 1: Literally the Worst 3
Entry 2: Moot Point vs. Mute Point 5
Entry 3: Me, Myself, and I (And My Confusion) 6
Entry 4: Their, There, They're 8
Entry 5: Affect vs. Effect 11
Entry 6: Who vs. Whom 14
Entry 7: Less vs. Fewer 17
Entry 8: Then vs. Than 20
Entry 9: Could Care Less 22
Entry 10: Bring vs. Take 24
Entry 11: Begging the Question 26
Entry 12: Enormity Isn't Just Enormous 28
Entry 13: Irony vs. Coincidence 30
Entry 14: Historic vs. Historical 32
Entry 15: Infer vs. Imply 34
Entry 16: Irregardless of Logic 36
Entry 17: Utilize vs. Use 38
Entry 18: Disinterested vs. Uninterested 40
Entry 19: Bemused vs. Amused 42
Entry 20: Anxious vs. Eager 44
Entry 21: Nauseous vs. Nauseated 46
Entry 22: To vs. Too (and Two, the Forgotten Middle Child) 48
Entry 24: Your vs. You're 50
Literally Too Many Words 52
The Ones That Got Away 54
That's All, Folks! 56

For Kirstan

Before We Begin: A Word About Words

Dear Reader,

Some people collect stamps. Others collect vinyl records. Me? I collect misused words. Not because I love them, but because they follow me everywhere like stray cats I never asked for. They show up in emails, headlines, text messages, and yes—even in books that should have known better. And every time I see one, a tiny part of me curls up inside and whispers, *Why are we like this?*

Let's be clear: I'm not talking about harmless typos. Everybody skips a letter now and then. I'm talking about the big offenders, the repeat criminals. Words that swagger into sentences pretending to belong, when in fact they've just stolen someone else's meaning and are waving it around like it's theirs. These aren't mistakes; they're full-blown word crimes.

Take *literally*. Once a proud and precise word, now it's forced to mean its exact opposite. Or *irregardless*, the zombie of the English language—slain by logic, only to rise again and lurch through dictionaries with a groan. Then there are the family feuds: *their/there/they're, to/too/two, your/you're*. Each one is an identity crisis waiting to happen.

Linguists have a term for this kind of mix-up: *malapropism*. It comes from a play written in the 1700s, where a character named Mrs. Malaprop kept mangling words. She'd call a pineapple a "polite apple," or say someone was the "very pineapple of politeness." Funny on stage. Less funny when your boss emails the whole office that "we must circumcise the problem immediately." (He meant *circumscribe*. At least, I hope he did.)

Malapropisms, eggcorns, overinflated vocabulary—English is crawling with them. And instead of rolling my eyes in silence (well, okay, I'll still do that), I've decided to document the chaos. Thus, this diary.

You won't find a dry textbook here. No charts, no quizzes, no wagging fingers. Just me, ranting about the daily absurdities of language, one misused word at a time. Some entries will be long and dramatic (because *literally* deserves nothing less). Others will be quick hits (looking at you, *moot point*). But all of them share the same mission: to poke fun at our messy, maddening, marvelous language.

Because here's the thing: I do love English. Deeply. It's flexible, inventive, always evolving. It lets us write poetry, crack jokes, and invent whole fantasy worlds. But it also trips over its shoelaces constantly, and someone has to laugh about it. Might as well be me.

So grab your red pen, your sense of humor, and maybe some aspirin. We're diving headfirst into the wild world of misused words. If you come out the other side a little wiser, great. If you just come out entertained, that's fine too.

Yours pedantically (and proudly),
The Writer Who Fights Word Crimes

Entry 1: Literally the Worst

Dear Diary,

"Literally" has trust issues. It was designed to mean *exactly what it says*—no exaggeration, no wiggle room. But now? It's the word people drag along to overblown claims all the time. "I literally died laughing." "My brain literally exploded." Unless the obituary section has resorted to stand-up comedy, that never happened.

The poor word is exhausted. It started life as a sturdy little adverb meaning "in a literal sense, <u>without metaphor</u>." You could count on it to keep things grounded. But over time, writers started getting cheeky. By the 1700s, even respectable authors were using it for emphasis. Jane Austen did it. Charles Dickens did it. F. Scott Fitzgerald even dropped a hyperbolic "literally" into *The Great Gatsby*. It's oddly comforting to know that when I complain about reality stars misusing it, I'm also shaking my fist at Dickens.

The trouble is, once dictionaries noticed this "figurative literally" sneaking around, they had a choice: wag their fingers and scold, or shrug and make it official. Guess which one they chose? Yep. Most dictionaries now list both meanings: the precise one, and the exaggerated one. Which means, Diary, that "literally" now officially means its opposite. I can't decide if that's linguistic evolution or the literary version of Stockholm syndrome.

What makes it worse is how casually people drop it into conversation. "I literally can't even." Do I call an ambulance? Or do I just hand them a snack and assume they mean "I'm mildly inconvenienced"? "I was literally glued to my seat." Really? Did the fire department have to come with solvent? "My boss literally bit my head off." In that case, I'd like to see the police report.

The sad part is, sometimes I almost do it myself. I'll be typing along and write "I literally flew through the air" when all I really did was stumble. And then my editor brain slams on the brakes. Backspace,

backspace. I can't let "literally" get away with exaggeration—it's like letting a toddler drive a car. Just because it *wants* to do something doesn't mean it should.

Of course, the language nerd in me knows that words shift meaning over time. "Awful" used to mean "awe-inspiring." "Nice" once meant "ignorant." "Egregious" used to be a compliment. Maybe "literally" is just going through its rebellious teenage years. But does it really need to turn into a double agent? Having a word mean one thing and its opposite is chaos, Diary. Pure chaos.

And then there's pop culture. Every sitcom character seems to sprinkle "literally" into their lines like it's parsley. Reality stars shout it across kitchens. Politicians pepper it into speeches. It's become filler, emphasis, drama—everything except what it was actually meant to be. Somewhere, the original definition is quietly weeping into its Oxford English Dictionary entry.

The truth is, "literally" is almost never necessary. If you say "I laughed until I cried," that's vivid enough. If you say "My brain exploded," people know it's a metaphor. We get it. And if you ever do find yourself in a situation where "literally" is required — like "I literally stepped on a Lego"—then, by all means, use it. You've earned it.

So yes, "literally" has become the poster child for misused words. I wish I could stage an intervention, hand it a blanket, and tell it to take a nap. But until then, every time I hear someone say "I literally can't live without my morning latte," I will quietly wish them good luck surviving the zombie apocalypse.

Yours exasperatedly,
The Writer Who Is Figuratively Dead Inside

Entry 2: Moot Point vs. Mute Point

Dear Diary,

    Today I stumbled across the phrase "mute point." Mute. As in silent. As in "this argument has lost its voice and will now be communicated via interpretive dance." I shouldn't laugh, but I do. A "mute point" sounds less like a debate and more like two people glaring at each other across a table in total silence.

    The phrase people usually want is "moot point." That's the original, borrowed from legal jargon. Back in the day, a "moot" was a meeting where lawyers-in-training argued hypothetical cases—debates with no real consequence. Over time, "moot point" came to mean "irrelevant" or "academic." But somewhere along the way, ears got confused, and "moot" slipped quietly into "mute."

    And honestly? I get it. "Moot" isn't a word we toss around much outside this one phrase. "Mute," on the other hand, shows up on TV remotes. People know mute. They don't know moot. So, when the brain has to choose between a dusty courtroom term and a button you press to shut up the commercials, it picks the button every time.

    Of course, once you picture it literally, it gets ridiculous. "That's a mute point" conjures an image of a lawyer standing up in court, opening his mouth with nothing coming out. Or two philosophers sitting across from each other, both holding up signs that read, "I disagree, but quietly." The whole debate is just one long awkward pause.

    So, here's the rule I intend to follow: it's "moot point" if I mean irrelevant, debatable, or academic. "Mute point" is just a typo in a Halloween costume. I might use it if I want to be funny—otherwise, I'll make my point loud and clear.

    Yours audibly,
The Writer Who Will Not Be Silenced

Entry 3: Me, Myself, and I (And My Confusion)

Dear Diary,

Sometimes I think pronouns are just out to mess with me. Especially *me, myself,* and *I*. They're like a dysfunctional trio of siblings who can't stop fighting in the back seat of the grammar car. "He and I went to the store." "He and me went to the store." "He and myself went to the store." Somewhere, an English teacher is weeping over her red pen.

Let's start with *I*. It's the golden child—the subject pronoun. *I went to the store.* Simple, straightforward. But throw another person into the sentence and suddenly things get dicey. "He and I went to the store" is fine, but people panic and swap *I* for *me*. Why? Because *me* feels friendlier, less formal, more natural. Unfortunately, it's also wrong in that context.

Then there's poor me. It's supposed to be the object—the one things happen to. Between you and me, that's perfectly normal. But when people try to sound fancy, they overcorrect. Suddenly it's, "Between you and I..." as if they've knighted themselves mid-sentence. "Sir I, Defender of Incorrect Grammar."

And then comes myself, the troublemaker. It's meant to do two jobs: reflexive (*I hurt myself*) or emphatic (*I baked the cake myself*). But somewhere along the way, myself decided it wanted a bigger career. Now it barges into sentences uninvited: *"If you have any questions, just talk to myself."* Or, even worse, *"John and myself are going to the store."* No, they are not. Myself is not a substitute for me, and it's not a fancier version of I. It's just confused.

The funniest part is how many professionals—politicians, CEOs, newscasters—fall into the trap. "Please contact John or myself if you have questions." They think it sounds polished. Really it sounds like John and *myself* don't know what we're talking about.

I get it, though. *I* feels too stiff. *Me* feels too casual. *Myself* feels like a safe middle ground. But grammar isn't about feelings; it's about function. And function says: *I* is for subjects, *me* is for objects, and *myself* is for when you're doing something to yourself.

Still, I catch myself hesitating sometimes. I'll type "between you and I" and then hear the ghosts of every English teacher I've ever had shrieking in unison. Backspace, backspace. It's "between you and me." Every. Single. Time.

I know I don't always get it right on the first try either. These three pronouns are sneaky. They show up at odd hours, switch places, and whisper bad advice. But when I finally untangle them and get it right, I feel like I deserve a medal. Or at least a slice of cake. That I baked myself.

Yours reflectively,

The Writer Who Keeps Fighting with Herself

Entry 4: Their, There, They're

Dear Diary,

If English were a family reunion, *their*, *there*, and *they're* would be the chaotic triplets no one can tell apart. They look vaguely similar, they keep borrowing each other's clothes, and everyone spends the whole afternoon calling the wrong one by the wrong name. Meanwhile, Grandma Grammar is clutching her pearls in the corner, muttering, "Why can't you children behave?"

Let's start with *their*. It's the possessive one. Think of it as the sibling who labels everything in the fridge: *their sandwich, their soda, their leftover pizza that mysteriously disappears anyway*. *Their* is the control freak, always clutching what belongs to someone. "That's their car." "Those are their shoes." "This is their problem, but somehow it's become mine." Simple, right?

Then we have *there*. This one is pointing at stuff. *There* is the kid who's always waving their arms around, shouting, "Over there! Look there!" It's all about place and existence. "The book is over there." "There is a hole in my sock." *There* is basically a living GPS unit, except it occasionally leads writers astray.

And finally, *they're*. The contraction. The social butterfly. Always pulling people together: *they are = they're*. This one gets invited everywhere but is constantly mistaken for its siblings. "They're going to the party" is perfectly fine. But the second you write "Their going to the party," you've invited the wrong triplet, and suddenly everyone's gossiping about your grammar behind your back.

When they show up together in the same sentence, it's the grammar equivalent of a perfectly choreographed ballet: *They're putting their books over there*. Mix even two of them up—*They're putting there books over their*—and you've got Three Stooges–level grammatical slapstick.

People say spelling mistakes don't matter much, and maybe that's true if you accidentally type "teh" instead of "the." Everyone knows what you mean. But mixing up *their, there, and they're*? That's different. It's a red flag on a dating profile, a dealbreaker in a job offer, the kind of thing that makes editors twitch like they've had too much coffee.

The internet, of course, has no mercy. Post a picture captioned "Their so cute!" and you'll get a thousand replies correcting you before you can hit edit. "*They're* so cute, actually." "Learn the difference!" "My eyes are bleeding!" Somewhere, an army of grammar vigilantes has nothing better to do than patrol comments like it's their civic duty.

But here's the secret shame, Diary: even I, the self-proclaimed word nerd, have tripped over these three in the dark. I'll be typing fast, lost in a sentence, and suddenly my fingers betray me. I type *there* when I mean *their*. I glance back and it's like finding I've put my shoes on the wrong feet. "How did that happen? Who let this slip past security?"

Sometimes, I wonder if the confusion is deliberate. Maybe the triplets get together at night and plot ways to ruin our prose. "Tomorrow, you sneak into that email," *their* says. "I'll hide in the middle of a sentence," *there* giggles. "And I'll just show up uninvited," *they're* adds, grinning like the class clown. And then off they go, wreaking havoc on unsuspecting writers.

The worst is when people try to justify the mistake. "You knew what I meant." Yes, but meaning isn't everything. If I show up to your house and say, "I brought you a desert," you'll be disappointed when it's sand instead of cake. Precision matters. That's why we have three different words in the first place.

I sometimes imagine them as triplets in therapy. *Their* is frustrated: "Everyone steals my stuff." *There* sighs: "No one listens when I point things out." *They're* interrupts: "They're just jealous because I'm the fun one." And the therapist, an overworked English teacher, takes another sip of coffee and pretends to write notes while plotting her escape.

The sad reality is, Diary, these three aren't going anywhere. They've been confusing people for centuries, and they'll keep doing it until the heat death of the universe. The best we can do is learn their quirks, practice a little extra caution, and maybe tattoo "They're = they are" on the inside of our eyelids.

So here's what I'm going to do: before I hit send, I will pause. If I wrote *their*, I ask, "Does it own something?" If I wrote *there*, I ask, "Is it pointing somewhere or existing?" If I wrote *they're*, I check if I can swap in *they are*. If not, I've grabbed the wrong triplet, and it's time to shove them back into the stroller where they belong.

Yours possessively, existentially, and socially,
The Writer Who Can Tell the Triplets Apart (Most Days)

Entry 5: Affect vs. Effect

Dear Diary,

Some words are meant to be together. Peanut butter and jelly. Salt and vinegar. Dragons and treasure. And then there are *affect* and *effect*—the dysfunctional couple of the English language. They've been in an on-again, off-again relationship for centuries, leaving chaos in their wake. Every time I think they've finally sorted things out, one storms off in a huff, the other slams the door, and I'm stuck explaining their drama to innocent bystanders.

Let's start with *affect*. It usually struts around as a verb, the one doing the action. "The weather affects my mood." "Coffee affects my ability to function." It's the mover, the shaker, the catalyst for change. *Affect* is always poking at things, stirring the pot, fiddling with emotions like it's auditioning for a daytime soap.

Then there's *effect*. This one usually shows up as a noun—the result, the outcome, the aftermath of *affect's* meddling. "The effect of coffee is alertness." "The effect of bad weather is me sulking in pajamas." If *affect* is the troublemaker, *effect* is the fallout. They're the reason you're picking glitter out of your carpet three months after the party.

Of course, just when you think you've got them pegged, they flip roles like untrustworthy actors. *Effect* occasionally moonlights as a verb ("to effect change"), meaning "to bring about." That's when it barges in wearing *affect's* clothes and confuses everyone. Meanwhile, *affect* sometimes tries on its serious psychologist costume, showing up as a noun ("a flat affect") to describe someone's emotional expression. At this point, I'm ready to hand them both a time-out and tell them to stop playing dress-up.

The real kicker is how close they look. They differ by a single letter, and both start with the same "uh" sound when you say them out loud. No wonder people trip over them like shoes left in a dark hallway. I once saw someone write: "The medicine effected me strongly." That poor sentence didn't know whether it was sick, cured, or in need of an intervention.

Sometimes I picture *affect* and *effect* as soap-opera characters. *Affect* is the dramatic lover, storming into the room shouting, "I'm changing your life forever!" Meanwhile, *effect* is lying on the chaise longue, sighing, "Yes, darling, and now look what you've done." Cue the dramatic organ music. They break up, make up, swap roles, and confuse everyone watching at home. It's like they are each other's evil twins.

The sad part, Diary, is that I still pause when I use them. I know the rules. I teach the rules. But mid-sentence, I'll freeze: "Is it affect or effect here?" Then comes the mental math. Verb? Probably *affect*. Noun? Probably *effect*. And if it's "to effect change," I mutter a small prayer and hope no one notices the sweat dripping off my forehead.

Here's the shortcut I cling to: **A is for action. E is for end result.** *Affect* acts. *Effect* ends. Simple enough, but the minute I relax, they sense my weakness and pounce.

The internet doesn't help. Half the articles out there misuse the pair so casually that even dictionaries seem to throw up their hands. "Fine," the lexicographers sigh. "If people insist on mangling the difference, we'll just add the alternate meaning." That's how *literally* wound up meaning its opposite, and it's how *affect* and *effect* are headed for permanent cohabitation in the same dictionary entry.

Then there's auto-correct, that hyper-vigilant ghost in the machine that was programmed by someone who doesn't actually know the difference between these two words. I swear there's a line of code in my phone that is the equivalent of a coin toss. Type "affect," and it smugly decides you meant "effect." Type "effect," and it switches it back to "affect." It's like a passive-aggressive roommate who keeps rearranging the furniture just to watch you trip.

I suppose part of the problem is that life is messy. Actions don't always have neat results. Sometimes there's no clear line between cause and consequence, and our words stumble trying to keep up. Maybe that's why *affect* and *effect* will never stop bickering—they're reflecting the human condition, one squabble at a time.

Still, Diary, I refuse to let them win. When I draft a sentence, I slow down, breathe, and double-check. "Did I mean the action or the outcome?" If I'm describing what's happening, it's *affect*. If I'm describing the result, it's *effect*. If I'm still not sure, I rephrase the whole thing until neither one can sneak in wearing a fake mustache.

Because at the end of the day, English may be messy, but I don't have to invite chaos into every sentence. And if *affect* and *effect* want to keep reenacting their soap opera, they can do it somewhere else—preferably off my page.

Yours dramatically,
The Writer Who Refuses to Be Affected by Their Effect

Entry 6: Who vs. Whom

Dear Diary,

If ever there was a word with a superiority complex, it's *whom*. He strolls in wearing a velvet smoking jacket, sipping brandy, and insisting you address him properly. Meanwhile, his cooler cousin *who* is leaning against the kitchen counter in ripped jeans, chatting up the guests. Nobody actually wants *whom* at the party, but he shows up anyway, sniffing at the hors d'oeuvres and reminding everyone of the "proper" way to eat canapés.

Here's the truth: *who* and *whom* are just subject and object pronouns. *Who* does the action, *whom* receives it. "Who ate the cake?" "To whom did you give the cake?" Simple enough. But in practice, nobody wants to play grammar detective every time cake is involved. So we mumble "who" and hope nobody notices.

Whom knows this, of course. That's why he acts so haughty—he's overcompensating. He used to be respectable, a regular guest at every formal sentence. "To whom it may concern." "For whom the bell tolls." But then casual English showed up in a t-shirt and sneakers, and suddenly *whom* was relegated to dusty legal letters and pretentious wedding invitations.

I'll admit, sometimes I try to sneak him in just to sound fancy. "Whom should I talk to about this problem?" It feels polished, elevated, like I've put on a suit just to send an email. But deep down, I know I'm faking it. Nine times out of ten, I'd rather write, "Who should I talk to?" and be done with it.

The rule itself is straightforward: if you can swap the word with *he* or *she*, use *who*. If you can swap with *him* or *her*, use *whom*. "Who is going to the party?" (*He is going to the party.*) "Whom should I invite?" (*I should invite him.*) The trick is remembering to run the test before your brain panics and defaults to cancelling the party altogether.

Of course, the internet complicates things. Half the time people use *whom* wrong in an effort to sound smarter. Politicians do it constantly. "Whom do you think will win the election?" they declare, proudly misusing the word in front of millions of viewers. Somewhere, an English teacher throws her shoe at the TV.

Even literature has betrayed us. Titles like *For Whom the Bell Tolls* have kept *whom* alive long past its natural expiration date. It's the reason it still shows up in customer service emails: "To whom it may concern." Concerned about what? My sanity? My dwindling patience? If you really cared, you'd just say, "Hello."

Sometimes I picture *who* and *whom* as estranged brothers. *Who* is the people's champion—easygoing, reliable, always ready to jump into a sentence without fuss. *Whom* is the snob, muttering about rules and respectability. They meet once a year at Thanksgiving, glare at each other across the table, and argue about who—pardon me, *whom*—Grandma loves more.

But the truth, Diary, is that English is slowly breaking up with *whom*. Most style guides admit it's fading from common usage. Even editors are starting to let it go unless the context is formal. That makes me oddly sad. I don't particularly like *whom,* but I'll miss the drama he brings to the page. It's like watching a villain get written out of the story. The story continues, but something is lost.

Still, I can't bring myself to use *whom* in casual writing. It's like showing up to a barbecue in a tuxedo. Everyone notices, but nobody's impressed. So my compromise is this: I save *whom* for the rare occasions when formality is expected—legal documents, academic papers, or that one pompous email where I need to feel superior. Everywhere else? *Who* gets the spotlight.

Because at the end of the day, clarity matters more than formality. If people roll their eyes at *whom,* the word has failed to do its job. So I'll let *who* keep mingling with the masses, while *whom* sulks in the corner with his brandy.

Yours informally,
The Writer Who Won't Invite Whom to the Party

Entry 7: Less vs. Fewer

Dear Diary,

If I had a nickel for every time I saw "10 items or less" at the grocery store, I'd have... well, *fewer* nickels than I'd like, but definitely *less* patience. This, Diary, is the hill I will die on: the difference between *less* and *fewer*. And judging by the number of checkout signs in the world, I'll be dying alone.

Here's the deal. *Fewer* is for things you can count: apples, nickels, dragons, annoying ex-boyfriends. *Less* is for stuff you can't count: water, air, patience, existential dread. It's not rocket science—it's literally first-grade math. "I have fewer marbles than you." "I have less sanity than yesterday." Countable vs. uncountable. Done.

But the world refuses to cooperate. Every time I walk into a store, the big sign above the express lane mocks me: "10 items or less." Less! As if *fewer* had been abducted by aliens and nobody noticed. I stand there, clutching my basket of frozen pizza and toothpaste, and imagine explaining to the cashier that "items" are countable. Ten bananas. Ten loaves of bread. Ten tubs of ice cream. Ten regrets. All countable. Therefore, *fewer*.

The irony, Diary, is that stores could fix this with one simple change: drop the number altogether. Just write "Express Lane." Or "Small Baskets Only." Or, if they're feeling sassy, "Don't test us with a full cart." Anything would be better than dangling that grammatically cursed "10 items or less" in our faces. But no, they insist on poking grammar nerds in the eye week after week. I sometimes think the sign-makers do it because they are following instructions on an order form and have lost the will to point it out to their customers.

Of course, language is slippery. There are times when *less* is perfectly fine with things that seem countable. Money, for instance. We say "less than ten dollars," not "fewer than ten dollars." Why? Because we're thinking of money as an uncountable mass, not individual coins. Same with time: "less than five minutes." You could technically count minutes, but we treat time as a flowing blob instead of individually wrapped minutes. Context is everything.

Still, the basic rule holds up most of the time: if you can count it, use *fewer*. If you can't, use *less*. "Fewer chairs in the room." "Less furniture in the room." Furniture is a collective blob. Chairs are for individual bottoms on which they will be seated.

What really gets me, Diary, is when people insist the rule doesn't matter. "Language evolves," they say. "Everyone says '10 items or less,' so it must be fine." To which I reply: everyone also eats pizza for breakfast sometimes, but that doesn't make it nutritionally correct. Just because a mistake is common doesn't mean we should hand it a medal.

Sometimes I picture *less* and *fewer* as rivals on a reality TV show. *Less* is the diva—bigger, flashier, hogging the spotlight. *Fewer* is the underdog, waving its hand from the sidelines, begging people to remember it exists. "I'm still here!" it cries, while *less* smirks and collects another paycheck. If *fewer* ever quits, I swear English will collapse under the weight of its own imprecision.

The funny part is that I don't even use the express lane that often. But just knowing the sign is there fills me with righteous indignation. I've daydreamed about sneaking into stores with a roll of correction stickers. "10 items or fewer," I'd plaster over the signs like some kind of grammar vigilante. Customers would nod in approval, and somewhere, an English teacher would feel a sudden rush of peace.

Until then, I take comfort in small victories. The BBC famously decreed that their news site would stick with "fewer" for countables, no matter what the masses say. If the Queen's English can hold the line, maybe all is not lost.

When in doubt, I ask myself if I can count it out loud. If yes, it's *fewer*. If no, it's *less*. If it's money or time, I'll just flip a coin and hope nobody emails me about it.

And if you see me in the grocery store express lane, glaring at the sign? Just know I'm not angry at you, Diary. I'm angry at the universe for letting *fewer* get trampled.

Yours with less patience and fewer friends after this rant,

The Writer Who Brings Too Many Items Through the Express Lane

Entry 8: Then vs. Than

Dear Diary,

Some words are sneaky because they look alike. Others because they sound alike. And then—*then!*—there's *than*. *Than* sneaks in, pretending to be *then's* twin and, just for fun they swap classes.

Here's the deal: *then* is about time. It's the next thing that happens. "We went to the store, then we went home." First A, then B. Cause and effect. Chronological order. It's the word that keeps things moving forward.

Than, on the other hand, is for comparisons. "Cake is better than pie." "I'd rather fight one dragon than twelve." It's the grammar referee holding up a measuring stick, showing which side wins. Without *than*, every argument would end in a confused tie.

Seems simple, right? And yet, Diary, people mix them up constantly. They write "I'd rather be happy then sad." No, you wouldn't. That means you plan to be happy first and sad afterward. Talk about a buzzkill. You wanted *than*. Or they'll write, "We went to dinner, than to the movie." Which makes it sound like dinner was a contestant in some kind of competition that no one knew they were participating in.

Sometimes I imagine *then* and *than* as rivals in a poetry slam. *Then* stands up and delivers a heartfelt timeline:

"I woke up, then I cried, then I drank coffee, then I thrived."

The crowd snaps politely.

Then *than* takes the mic, all attitude:

"My poem is shorter than yours. My rhymes are sharper than swords. I am greater than thee!"

The crowd goes wild.

They're both strong performers, but swap them mid-line and the whole thing falls apart. "I am greater then thee" just sounds like bad Shakespearean fanfic.

I admit I've caught myself tripping over them, especially when typing fast. They're only one letter apart, and spellcheck never cares. You can write "better then" all day and your word processor will shrug like, "Looks good to me." Meanwhile, I'm left rereading the sentence, wondering why it feels wrong.

Whenever I spot a *then/than* situation, I stop and ask—am I talking about **time** or **comparison**? If it's time, I grab *then*. If it's comparison, I grab *than*. And if I'm still unsure, I rewrite the sentence before either one can drag me into bad-poetry territory.

Because the truth is, Diary, these words deserve better than being swapped like identical twins in a sitcom. They each have their role. *Then* is the storyteller. *Than* is the judge. Mix them up, and suddenly your meaning is muddier than swamp water.

Yours comparably,
The Writer Who Would Rather Get It Right Than Wrong

Entry 9: Could Care Less

Dear Diary,

Few phrases make me grind my teeth harder than "I could care less." People toss it into conversation as if it means they don't give a flying fig about the topic. But think about it: if you *could* care less, that means you still care at least a little. You've got wiggle room on the caring scale. The phrase you're actually looking for is "I *couldn't* care less." Zero. Nada. The bottom of the caring barrel.

It's like someone saying, "I could stand to eat more cake." Great, that means you haven't hit your limit yet. Or, "I could be more annoyed." Congratulations, you're admitting you're only halfway to fury. Saying "I could care less" is not the indifference power move people think it is. It's more like bragging, "Behold, I still care enough to spare some!"

Where did this mangled phrase come from? Nobody's quite sure. Some linguists think it started as sarcasm—people deliberately dropping the "n't" to make the point even snarkier. "Oh sure, I could care less." Wink, wink. But over time, the sarcasm vanished, and we were left with a phrase that means the opposite of what people think it means. English does love its little pranks.

Still, it drives me up the wall. Imagine a breakup scene:

"I don't love you anymore. In fact, I could care less."

"Well thank you, darling, for letting me know I still rank somewhere above moldy cheese."

The worst part is how widespread it's become. I hear it in TV shows, in movies, in political speeches. Entire crowds cheer along, none the wiser that they're technically proclaiming a tiny flicker of concern. It's like a linguistic group hug nobody asked for.

But here's the thing, Diary: language lives in the wild, not just in grammar books. If enough people use a phrase wrong for long enough, it becomes "right" by sheer force of repetition. "Could care less" has been around for decades, and it shows no signs of packing its bags. So maybe I should save my blood pressure and let the masses keep their almost-indifference.

Not today, though. Today, I'm holding the line. If I truly don't care, I *couldn't* care less. Period. And if someone says they *could* care less, I'll just smile sweetly and ask, "Oh really? How much less could you care?"

Yours apathetically,
The Writer Who Couldn't Care Less (and Means It)

Entry 10: Bring vs. Take

Dear Diary,

Some words are like squabbling roommates, forever arguing about directions. *Bring* and *take* are locked in this domestic comedy, shouting across the apartment:

"Bring it here!"

"No, take it there!"

And somewhere in the middle, the poor object just wants to know which way it's supposed to go.

The rule, in theory, is simple. *Bring* means movement **toward** the speaker. *Take* means movement **away.** "Bring me the book." (Toward me.) "Take the book to Sarah." (Away from me.) That's it. We're just playing follow-the-arrows.

But people blur the lines all the time. "I'll bring it to your house later." Technically, you're taking it to their house, because you're moving it away from your location. The only way you're "bringing" it is if you're already there, standing in their living room, yelling through the phone. Otherwise, it's *take*.

Why does this trip us up so much? Probably because we're used to speaking from other people's perspectives. If I'm on the phone with Sarah and I say, "I'll bring the book to your house," I'm thinking about her point of view. By the time I get there, the book will indeed be "brought." But right now, in my current spot, the correct word is *take*. It's like a grammar tug-of-war between the here-and-now and the future-there.

Sometimes I imagine *bring* and *take* as a couple arguing in the car. *Bring* insists on heading home, while *take* just wants to go on a road trip. The poor driver (me) just bangs the steering wheel and screams, "Decide already!" Meanwhile, the map app is no help—it's still trying to reroute me around construction.

The difference does matter, though. Precision keeps your sentences clear. "Bring your homework to class" makes sense because the class is the destination where both speaker and listener will be. "Take your homework home" is equally clear—it's leaving you with the student. If you muddle them, you risk leaving your poor homework stranded somewhere in between, like a sad notebook hitchhiking on the highway.

Of course, plenty of people don't care. They swap the words freely, and everyone usually understands what they mean. Context does a lot of heavy lifting. But every time I hear "I'll bring it there," a little part of me wants to shout, "But you're not there yet!"

If it's coming toward me, it's *bring*. If it's going away from me, it's *take*. Easy enough—though I'll admit I still slip sometimes. After all, Diary, words don't just travel across paper. They travel across perspectives, and sometimes they forget to update their luggage tags.

Yours directionally,

The Writer Who Takes Things Too Far and Brings Them Up Anyway

Entry 11: Begging the Question

Dear Diary,

Few phrases are as tragically misunderstood as "begging the question." People toss it around like it means "this raises the question," but that's not what it was born to do. Somewhere out there, a philosophy professor is weeping in his tweed jacket every time a newscaster says, "That begs the question: what happens next?"

The original meaning comes from logic—fancy, syllogism-loving logic. "Begging the question" is a type of circular reasoning where the argument assumes its own conclusion. Like saying, "Ghosts exist because I saw a ghost." Or, "This medicine works because it's effective." Nothing is proven; it's just the same idea dancing around in a circle.

That's the true "begging the question." It's not about raising a new question—it's about dodging the answer. Yet modern English has latched onto the mistaken version with the enthusiasm of a toddler grabbing candy. "That begs the question: what will the stock market do?" No, that *raises* the question. It doesn't beg anything except maybe forgiveness.

Sometimes I imagine the phrase itself sulking in the corner. "I used to mean something important!" it cries. "I was a shining example of logical fallacy! And now people use me when they mean 'by the way...'" Poor thing. If idioms could drink, this one would be halfway through a bottle of cheap wine, singing bad karaoke.

I'll admit, Diary, I've slipped myself. It's so tempting—"begs the question" has a nice rhythm, and everyone knows what you mean in the modern sense. But every time I type it, my inner editor slaps my hand and whispers, "That's not what it means, and you know it." Backspace, backspace. I swap in "raises the question" and carry on.

Will the misuse eventually become the official definition? Probably. Dictionaries are already sighing and adding it as a secondary meaning. Language is democratic that way: if enough people break the rule, the rule changes. But part of me will always mourn the original, precise version—the one that guarded us against sloppy arguments.

So, Diary, here's my stance: if I'm making a logical point, I'll save "begging the question" for circular reasoning. If I just want to bring something up, I'll say "raises the question." And if I come across it in the wild? I won't beg. I'll just roll my eyes and pour another cup of coffee.

Yours logically,
The Writer Who Refuses to Go in Circles

Entry 12: Enormity Isn't Just Enormous

Dear Diary,

Some words were never meant for burritos. *Enormity* is one of them. And yet, every week I see headlines like: "The Enormity of the Sandwich Challenge!" or "The Enormity of My Netflix Queue." No, Diary. Just... no. *Enormity* isn't a supersized synonym for *enormous*. It's not about big burritos, long to-do lists, or skyscrapers taller than my ambitions.

The true meaning of *enormity* is *great evil, wickedness, or moral horror*. The enormity of genocide. The enormity of a war crime. The enormity of human cruelty. It's not about size—it's about seriousness. When you say "the enormity of my laundry pile," you're essentially comparing dirty socks to atrocities. Hyperbolic, sure, but also a little tone-deaf.

I sometimes picture *enormity* sitting in a dark cloak, scowling at the frivolous company it's forced to keep. "I was meant to describe the unspeakable," it mutters. "Not the portion size at a Tex-Mex restaurant." Meanwhile, *enormous* lounges on the couch, popping popcorn. "Lighten up, bro. People just like me better."

To be fair, dictionaries have started to blur the lines. Enough people misuse *enormity* that modern lexicons now list "hugeness" as an alternate definition. The purists wail, but the tide is hard to stop once it's rolling. Still, I can't help wincing. Using *enormity* to mean "big" feels like putting on a hazmat suit just to clean the garage. Technically plausible, but awkward for everyone involved.

Sometimes I think writers reach for *enormity* because it sounds fancier than *enormous*. It's the same impulse that makes people say *utilize* instead of *use*. There's a misguided belief that longer syllables equal smarter prose. But trust me, nobody's impressed when you describe your cat's furball as an "enormity." They're just wondering if you need counseling.

When I mean big, I say *enormous*. If I mean evil, I say *enormity*. Easy. No burrito atrocities. No genocidal sock piles. Just clarity.

The sad truth is, *enormity* will probably keep sliding toward "big" until that's all it means. But until the day it gives up its gravitas completely, I'll defend its darker, heavier weight. English has plenty of words for size. Let's keep this one for the moments that deserve it.

Yours monstrously,
The Writer Who Thinks Burritos Deserve Better

Entry 13: Irony vs. Coincidence

Dear Diary,

If I had a dime for every time someone shouted, "That's ironic!" when they really meant "That's a coincidence," I'd have enough to retire on a small island. Ironically—or perhaps coincidentally—it would probably rain the day I arrived. And somewhere, Alanis Morissette would be nodding knowingly.

Let's get one thing straight: **coincidence** is when two unrelated things happen at the same time by chance. You bump into your old college roommate at a gas station in Saskatchewan? Coincidence. You and your coworker show up wearing the same shirt? Coincidence. Mildly amusing, occasionally awkward, but not ironic.

Irony, on the other hand, is about expectations colliding with reality. It's when the outcome is the opposite of what you'd expect. A fire station burning down. A marriage counselor filing for divorce. A spelling bee champion misspelling "grammar." That's irony. It stings a little. It has bite.

The problem, Diary, is that irony is tricky. Even smart people get tangled up in its definitions. There's situational irony (events turn out the opposite of what you'd think), dramatic irony (when the audience knows something the character doesn't), and verbal irony (basically sarcasm with better PR). That's a lot of categories to juggle while also trying to decide if rain on your wedding day qualifies.

Spoiler: it doesn't. Rain on your wedding day is just bad weather. Unless, of course, you're marrying a meteorologist who swore it would be sunny, in which case, yes, we're edging into irony territory.

Poor Alanis. Her song "Ironic" gave us a generation of people convinced that traffic jams and free rides when you've already paid are dripping with irony. They're not. They're just unfortunate timing. If she'd called the song "Coincidental," it wouldn't have sold as many albums, but English teachers everywhere would have slept better at night.

I sometimes imagine irony and coincidence as rival lawyers in a courtroom. Coincidence strolls in, shrugging. "Hey, weird stuff happens." Irony storms in with dramatic flair: "Objection! This is the opposite of what anyone expected!" The jury, confused, just wants to go home, so they call everything irony and move on.

Of course, language evolves, and misuse piles up until dictionaries surrender. These days, many dictionaries list "coincidence" as part of irony's definition because so many people blur the line. But every time I hear someone say, "Isn't it ironic we ran into each other here?" I feel like shouting, "No, Brenda, it's a coincidence. Unless you were deliberately trying to avoid me and fate punished you here—then we'll talk irony."

The funny thing is, irony is everywhere once you know how to spot it. The dentist with cavities. The pilot afraid of heights. The English teacher who spells "definitely" as "defiantly" in a Facebook post. That's the delicious sting of irony: it exposes our little contradictions. Coincidence, by contrast, is harmless. It's life's random dice roll.

Whenever I'm tempted to call something ironic, I stop and ask: **Did this turn out the opposite of what was expected?** If yes, irony. If not, coincidence. It's a simple filter that saves me from embarrassing myself in front of English professors—and Alanis fans with strong opinions.

Because the truth is, Diary, irony deserves respect. It's not just a quirky label for anything unexpected. It's a literary device, a storytelling tool, a mirror held up to human folly. Coincidence can make me chuckle. Irony can make me wince. And sometimes, if it's sharp enough, irony can make me laugh and cry at the same time.

So, the next time someone points to a traffic jam on their way to work and sighs, "How ironic," I'll just pat them on the shoulder and say, "No, dear. It's Tuesday."

Yours sarcastically,
The Writer Who Knows Coincidence When She Sees It

Entry 14: Historic vs. Historical

Dear Diary,

Every old building wants to be called *historic*. The leaning barn down the road? "Historic." That coffee shop that opened in 2019 but has a chalkboard wall? Also "historic." Somewhere in the distance, actual historians are banging their heads against filing cabinets.

Here's the difference: *historic* means "important in history." The signing of the Declaration of Independence? Historic. The moon landing? Historic. That time I ate an entire cheesecake by myself? Not historic—though possibly *heroic*.

Historical, on the other hand, simply means "related to history." A historical novel is set in the past. A historical society studies old records. A historical costume makes you look like you've time-traveled from the 1800s. *Historical* is descriptive. *Historic* is evaluative. One points backward; the other bestows significance.

But people blur them constantly. I once heard someone call their neighbor's basement "a historic rec room" because it still had shag carpet from the 70s. That's not historic, Diary. That's just unfortunate interior design.

Sometimes I picture *historic* and *historical* as two tour guides. *Historic* strides out in a top hat, booming: "This site changed the world!" Meanwhile, *historical* follows quietly, pointing at dusty ledgers: "This site had plumbing installed in 1847." Both useful. Both valid. But they're not interchangeable.

The misuse really matters in writing. If a politician calls their speech *historic,* they're declaring it world-changing. If a journalist calls it *historical,* they're just saying it relates to the past. Subtle difference, huge implications. Imagine the confusion if the local library announced a "Historic Fiction Book Club." Do I show up expecting novels that changed the world, or do I wear bell bottoms? The wrong word sends readers to the wrong shelf.

The tragedy, Diary, is that *historic* gets overinflated. Everything is labeled historic now—sports games, first dates, pumpkin spice latte season. The more we use it carelessly, the less weight it carries when something truly deserves it. If everything is historic, nothing is.

What it all comes down to is: if it shaped history, call it *historic;* and if it merely relates to history, call it *historical.* And if it's just my uncle's basement bar from 1978, call it "retro" and move on.

Because words, like buildings, deserve care. Some are ornate and important; others are just old and drafty. Confusing the two? That's not historic—it's just sloppy.

Yours significantly,
The Writer Who Knows a Historic Moment When She Sees One

Entry 15: Infer vs. Imply

Dear Diary,

Some conversations are like bad improv—one person says something, the other person misinterprets it, and suddenly you're arguing about the price of pineapples. At the root of the chaos? *Infer* and *imply*. These two love to play the blame game, and writers are forever caught in the crossfire.

Here's the difference: *imply* is what the speaker does. They hint, they suggest, they drop breadcrumbs. *Infer* is what the listener does. They pick up those breadcrumbs and decide they've found the trail to Grandma's house, when really it just led to the neighbor's garage.

Example: If I say, "It's getting late," I'm implying that you should probably leave. If you hear me and think, "She wants me gone," you're inferring. Imply = send. Infer = receive. Simple, right? And yet people swap them constantly, like mismatched socks.

I once heard a politician say, "I would like to infer that my opponent is lying." No, sir. You'd like to *imply* it. The opponent's supporters might infer it. What you're actually doing is revealing that your campaign speechwriters need a stern talking-to.

Sometimes I picture *imply* and *infer* as shady characters in a crime drama. *Imply* slips a note under the table: "Meet me at midnight." *Infer* reads it and concludes, "Clearly this means we're robbing a bank." Cue the car chase, the confusion, and the inevitable grammar police sirens.

The problem is that implication and inference are so tightly linked that people forget which side of the exchange they're on. Imply feels fancier, so it gets overused. Infer sounds intellectual, so people drop it in when they're trying to impress. Both end up mangled.

The misuse isn't just pedantic nitpicking, either—it can flip meaning. If a scientist says, "We can infer from the data," that means the evidence suggests a conclusion. If they say, "We can imply by the data," it sounds like the data is whispering secrets in the lab. Different jobs, different directions.

To keep them straight, I imagine a game of catch. The speaker *throws* the ball (implies). The listener *catches* the ball (infers). If you say "I inferred that," you're admitting you picked up the hint. If you say "I implied that," you're admitting you dropped it in the first place. And if you say both, you're just playing catch with yourself, which looks weird in public.

In the end, Diary, *imply* and *infer* are a team. One sets the stage, the other reads between the lines. The trouble comes when they swap scripts. So I'll keep reminding myself: I imply. You infer. And together, we misunderstand each other beautifully.

Yours suggestively (but not too much),
The Writer Who Trusts You to Infer Correctly

Entry 16: Irregardless of Logic

Dear Diary,

Few words are as universally mocked and yet stubbornly alive as *irregardless*. Every time it pops up in conversation, I feel the ghost of my high school English teacher materializing behind me, brandishing a red pen. "It's not a word!" she hisses. Except—it is. Sort of. Dictionaries, tired of fighting, now list it with a resigned shrug.

The problem is baked right into the word. *Regardless* already means "without regard." Slap an *ir-* on the front and you're basically saying "without without regard." A double negative in a trench coat, sneaking past the bouncers of logic. By that reasoning, *irregardless* should mean the opposite of *regardless,* but it doesn't. It means the same thing. English, explain yourself.

Some argue that *irregardless* is just folksy emphasis, the linguistic equivalent of adding an extra "real" in "really real." Others insist it's an ugly accident that refuses to die, like a zombie shambling through the dictionary. The truth? It's been around for over a century. Newspapers used it in the early 1900s. Politicians said it into microphones. By now, it's too late to bury it. The monster has citizenship.

Still, every time I hear it, I picture *regardless* and *irregardless* glaring at each other across a table. *Regardless* is sharp, concise, confident. *Irregardless* is the embarrassing sibling who tags along, insisting they belong. "I mean the same thing!" it yells. "Why are you even here?" *Regardless* snaps back. Meanwhile, the rest of us sip our drinks uncomfortably, pretending we don't hear them.

What really gets me, Diary, is how people use *irregardless* as if it sounds fancier than *regardless.* They think it has extra gravitas, like it's wearing a bow tie. In reality, it's more like showing up to a black-tie event in a tuxedo T-shirt. Sure, you might get in the door, but everyone will be side-eyeing you.

To be fair, most dictionaries now include *irregardless,* but usually with a note: "nonstandard" or "use regardless instead." Which is basically the lexicographical equivalent of an eye-roll. The word is there because people use it, not because it's beloved. Even Merriam-Webster, ever the realist, sighs and admits defeat: "Yes, fine, it exists. But maybe don't."

I'll admit, I've slipped once or twice, usually mid-rant. "Irregardless of the facts—wait, no, regardless of the facts—ugh." The word is sneaky that way, slipping into your mouth when you're worked up and not paying attention. Like a linguistic photobomber, it leaps into the frame just as the picture's being taken.

So what's the verdict? Technically, *irregardless* is a word. But it's also a word that makes half the audience twitch and the other half get all judgy. Why risk it? *Regardless* does the job beautifully, no double negatives required. Writers need to save *irregardless* for comedy sketches, ironic tweets, or moments when they want to watch their editor's blood pressure spike.

At the end of the day, words aren't just about being understood. They're about being respected. And *irregardless* may have earned a spot in the dictionary, but it'll never earn my respect.

Yours redundantly,
The Writer Who Will Never Regard Irregardless

Entry 17: Utilize vs. Use

Dear Diary,

If ever there were a word that strutted around in a tuxedo when jeans would do, it's *utilize*. People love it because it sounds smarter than *use*, like the difference between fine dining and heating leftovers in the microwave. But let's be honest: nine times out of ten, *utilize* is just an overdressed stand-in for plain old *use*.

The truth is, *utilize* has a narrower meaning. It's meant for making practical use of something in a way it wasn't originally intended. "We utilized the shoebox as a filing cabinet." That makes sense—you're repurposing the shoebox. But saying, "I utilized a spoon to eat my cereal," makes breakfast sound like a government grant proposal.

I once heard a coworker say, "We need to utilize our resources better." What he really meant was, "Use them." But *utilize* gave it that extra veneer of importance, as if we were about to invent cold fusion instead of reorganizing the supply closet. It's linguistic inflation—like calling your cat "feline domestic companion" when "cat" works fine.

Sometimes I picture *use* and *utilize* as siblings. *Use* is practical, down-to-earth, always getting the job done. *Utilize* is the pretentious older brother who studied abroad one semester and won't stop reminding everyone about it. "Ah yes, I once utilized a scooter to traverse the cobblestone streets of Prague." Relax, Chad. You used it. Calm down.

Of course, dictionaries now accept the casual use of *utilize* as a synonym for *use*, because people keep writing it into resumes, corporate memos, and college essays. But every time I see it, I wonder if the writer thinks it'll earn them extra credit. Spoiler: it won't. It just makes the sentence heavier, clunkier, and slightly ridiculous.

When plain old *use* works, I stick with it and save *utilize* for the rare times when I'm describing an unusual or resourceful application of something. Otherwise, I'm just dressing my sentence in unnecessary sequins.

Because clarity, Diary, is more important than ego. And the truth is, "use" has done the job perfectly well for centuries. It doesn't need a showy big brother horning in on the action.

Yours practically,
The Writer Who Uses Words, Not Utilizes Them

Entry 18: Disinterested vs. Uninterested

Dear Diary,

There are mix-ups that make me laugh, and then there are mix-ups that make me want to bang a gavel. *Disinterested* and *uninterested* fall firmly in the second category. They look like twins, but they're playing entirely different roles in the courtroom of English.

Disinterested doesn't mean bored. It means impartial, unbiased, having no personal stake in the matter. Think of a judge who doesn't care which side wins because their only job is to be fair. That's disinterested. In fact, in many contexts, it's a compliment: "The committee was disinterested." Translation: they weren't bribed with gift cards or free muffins; they weighed the evidence fairly.

Uninterested, meanwhile, is the word you want when you mean bored, indifferent, or about to fall asleep. "The audience looked uninterested." "My cat was uninterested in my poetry reading." That's the shrug, the yawn, the glazed expression during a staff meeting.

But oh, how often do people swap them! I once heard someone say, "The referee was disinterested in the game." What they meant was *uninterested*—the guy was daydreaming about tacos instead of watching the ball. Instead, they accidentally suggested the ref was gloriously impartial, which is the literal job description. Not quite the slam they thought it was.

I like to think of *disinterested* and *uninterested* as lawyers arguing over definitions. *Disinterested* stands tall, briefcase in hand: "I object to bias and favoritism." *Uninterested* slouches in the back row, scrolling Instagram: "Whatever, man. I couldn't care less." They're not even competing in the same trial, yet people keep confusing them.

The misuse isn't harmless, either. In legal, political, or academic contexts, the distinction matters. A *disinterested* mediator is exactly what you want. An *uninterested* mediator is a disaster who's doodling on a legal pad while your ex is getting the house, the boat, the vacation home, half your pension, and the dog. Precision saves more than grammar—it saves dignity.

A quick test writers can use to determine which word works best is: if you mean "fair and neutral," use *disinterested*. If you mean "bored stiff," use *uninterested*. And if you're unsure, ask yourself: does this person have a neutral stance, or do they not care at all? There's your answer.

Because at the end of the day, Diary, these two words deserve better than being tossed around interchangeably. One holds the scales of justice. The other holds a pillow and a blanket. Confuse them, and you've turned the courtroom into a nap room.

Yours impartially,

The Writer Who Is Never Uninterested in Grammar

Entry 19: Bemused vs. Amused

Dear Diary,

Every now and then, I stumble across a sentence like: *"She was bemused by the comedian's antics."* The writer thinks they're saying she was entertained. Nope. If she was bemused, she wasn't laughing—she was confused, probably staring at the stage like the comedian had just sprouted antlers. *Amused* is laughter. *Bemused* is bewilderment. Mix them up, and your character goes from giggling to baffled in one misplaced syllable.

That's the trap: *bemused* sounds like it ought to be the moody cousin of *amused,* all giggles with a hint of sophistication. In reality, it lives in a completely different neighborhood. If you're bemused by a joke, you didn't get it—you're the one blinking in silence while everyone else is rolling in the aisles.

I sometimes see them as theater critics. *Amused* is in the front row, laughing at every pratfall, applauding between acts, throwing roses on the stage. *Bemused* is in the balcony, squinting at the program notes, muttering, "Wait, is this a tragedy or a comedy? Why are there spoons involved?" Two very different reviews of the same play.

The misuse is so common that even respected publications blur the line. I once read a novel where the hero described his date as "bemused" by his wit. What was actually saying was: "She was deeply confused by everything I said." Which, to be fair, might have been accurate. The hero, however, seemed to be the confused one.

It's a subtle distinction, but it matters. If you say you were *amused* by the magician, I know you laughed at the tricks. If you say you were *bemused,* I picture you frowning at the disappearing rabbit, wondering if animal control should get involved. Precision paints the right picture—and saves writers from unintentionally calling their friends clueless.

So here's my rule: if I mean entertained, I go with *amused*. If I mean perplexed, I go with *bemused*. And if I'm both at once—which, let's be honest, happens often—I'll just say, "I was laughing and confused," and let the dictionary sort itself out.

Because, Diary, words don't have to be fancy to be right. Sometimes plain clarity is funnier than all the bemusement in the world.

Yours clearly entertained,

The Writer Who Finds Confusion Less Funny Than Comedy

Entry 20: Anxious vs. Eager

Dear Diary,

If someone tells me they're "anxious to go to Disneyland," I'll start picturing them clutching a paper bag, hyperventilating while in the line for Space Mountain. That's because *anxious* isn't supposed to mean excited—it means worried, nervous, full of dread. If Mickey Mouse gives you anxiety, by all means, go with *anxious*. But if you're simply bouncing in your seat with anticipation, what you mean is *eager*.

It's a subtle shift, but the words carry very different baggage. *Eager* is bright-eyed, ready, practically wagging its tail. "I'm eager to start my new job." *Anxious* is pacing the floor, biting its nails. "I'm anxious about starting my new job." See? One's all sunshine and rainbows; the other is storm clouds and acid reflux.

I sometimes imagine *anxious* and *eager* as siblings on a road trip. *Eager* is in the front seat shouting, "Are we there yet?" every five minutes, full of energy. *Anxious* is in the back seat, whispering, "What if the car breaks down? What if we hit traffic? What if the hotel loses our reservation?" Both are anticipating the trip, but only one is enjoying it.

So how did *anxious* sneak into *eager's* territory? Blame sloppy usage over time. People wanted a fancier way to say "excited," so they grabbed *anxious* and wore it like a sparkly jacket. Dictionaries, in their usual "fine, whatever" fashion, eventually added the "eager" sense as a secondary definition. But purists still twitch every time they hear it.

Context is everything. If I say, "She was anxious to meet her blind date," do I mean she was excited, or that she was worried he'd be a serial killer? The ambiguity can make writing wobble. Swap in *eager* for positive anticipation. Leave *anxious* for dread.

Of course, I slip too. I'll type "I'm anxious to get started" in an email, and then wonder if my client thinks I'm nervous about editing their manuscript. Cue me backspacing anxiously muttering, "No, I'm *eager*. I'm eager, dang it."

A simple way to look at it is: if your heart is racing in a good way, say *eager*. If it's racing in a bad way, say *anxious*. And if it's both—well, welcome to adulthood.

Yours eagerly (but not anxiously),
The Writer Who Has Butterflies Either Way

Entry 21: Nauseous vs. Nauseated

Dear Diary,

Few misuses make me queasier than when someone mixes up nauseous and nauseated. People say "I feel nauseous" when what they really mean is "I feel *nauseated*." Here's the difference: *nauseous* means "causing nausea." *Nauseated* means "feeling sick." If you're nauseous, technically you're the problem. If you're nauseated, you've got the problem.

Picture it this way: *"That smell is nauseous."* Translation: it's making other people gag. *"I feel nauseated."* Translation: I'm the one gagging. Swap them, and suddenly you're announcing to the world that you, personally, are human toxic waste. Not exactly the impression you want at a dinner party.

Of course, English being English, the misuse has become so widespread that dictionaries now list "feeling sick" under *nauseous*. Which means, yes, you can get away with it. But every time someone says "I feel nauseous," a pedant somewhere rolls their eyes and mutters, "No, darling, *you* are not nauseous—you are nauseated." And then they adjust their pearls before fainting dramatically on a chaise lounge.

I once saw a doctor on TV solemnly announce, "My patient was nauseous." All I could think was: *poor guy, even his doctor found him repulsive.* The patient, meanwhile, was probably too nauseated to care.

The real problem is that *nauseated* just doesn't sound as nice. It's clunky, heavy, the linguistic equivalent of a brick. *Nauseous* is sleek, stylish, easy to say. No wonder people reach for it first, even if it technically flips the meaning.

Still, I cling to the original distinction, because it's deliciously precise. If the roller coaster made me sick, I was *nauseated*. If the roller coaster itself was hideous enough to make other people sick, then it was *nauseous*. One describes my stomach. The other describes the monstrosity of a carnival ride that should have been shut down in 1983.

So, when I'm the one feeling ill, I say *nauseated*. When something else is disgusting enough to make people ill, I say *nauseous*. And if I hear someone use them interchangeably? Well, Diary, I'll just smile weakly and ask where the nearest bathroom is.

Yours queasily,
The Writer Who Is Trying Not to Hurl

Entry 22: To vs. Too (and Two, the Forgotten Middle Child)

Dear Diary,

    Few things make me want to throw my keyboard out the window faster than seeing *to* and *too* swapped around like mismatched mittens. And poor *two*—the innocent bystander—gets dragged into the mess just because it happens to sound the same. Three tiny words, one giant headache.

    Let's break it down. *To* is the workhorse—our preposition pal, always pointing somewhere or marking an infinitive. "I'm going to the store." "I like to read." Without *to*, half our sentences would collapse like sad soufflés.

    Too is the dramatic sibling. It means "also" or "excessively," and it always shows up with a little extra flair. "I want to come too!" or "That chicken wrap is too big for one person." (Though let's be honest, I'm still going to try.)

    And then there's poor *two*, the neglected middle child. It's just a number, quietly doing math homework in the corner while its siblings hog the spotlight. It doesn't often get misused, but I think that makes it a little smug too.

    The trouble comes when people mash them up in writing. I once saw a social media post that read, "I want ice cream to." Missing that extra *o* made it sound like the writer had cut their thought in half—ice cream to... what? Stay in the freezer? Hit the floor? Add the *o*, and it suddenly makes sense: "I want ice cream too." Same sentence, one tiny letter, completely different meaning.

    Or there's the classic text message: "I love you to." To what? To the moon? To be on time? To walk the neighbor's dog? Without the extra *o*, it sounds like you quit halfway through your affection. Add the *o*, and suddenly it's whole: "I love you too." Romance restored. Break up text averted.

Sometimes I imagine these three words as siblings in a family drama. *To* is the overworked parent, driving everyone around. *Too* is the attention-seeker, constantly shouting "Me too! Me too!" And *two* just sighs and mutters, "I think I was adopted?"

The good news is, the fix is simple. If I mean direction or an infinitive, it's *to*. If I mean "also" or "excessively," it's *too*. If I'm doing math, it's *two*. Quick test: swap *too* for "also." If the sentence still makes sense... Nailed it! "I want ice cream too." Yep. "I'm going too the store." Nope—not even if I'm very enthusiastic about the store.

So, Diary, I'll keep fighting the good fight. Because life's too short, grammar's too messy, and I only have two hands to fix all these errors. But I'll do what I can.

Yours excessively,
The Writer Who Loves Grammar Too Much

Entry 24: Your vs. You're

Dear Diary,

If there's one mistake guaranteed to spark a comment war online, it's *your* vs. *you're*. Forget politics, religion, or pineapple on pizza—this is the hill Facebook users actually die on.

The difference should be simple. *Your* is possessive. It means something belongs to you: *your book, your cat, your questionable life choices.* *You're* is a contraction of *you are.* *You're late. You're amazing. You're not going to believe how many times people mess this up.*

But simple doesn't mean safe. People swap them constantly. I once saw a bumper sticker that read: "Your Beautiful." Which made me want to pull up next to the driver and shout, "MY beautiful what? Car? Shoes? Grammar rage?" What they meant, of course, was *You're beautiful.* The sentiment was sweet, but the missing apostrophe turned it into a head-scratcher.

I can see *your* and *you're* as actors who keep getting miscast. *Your* is the prop master, always assigning ownership: "Here's your pen, your script, your spotlight." *You're* is the leading role, stepping onto the stage with presence: "You're ready. You're brilliant. You're going to nail this performance." Mix them up, and suddenly the prop master is trying to deliver the soliloquy while the star of the show is stuck handing out pencils. Chaos.

Part of the problem is speed. People type fast, autocorrect shrugs, and suddenly entire arguments collapse under the weight of the wrong form. "Your wrong" instead of "You're wrong." It's like showing up to a duel with a rubber chicken. You might have had a good point, but nobody's going to take you seriously.

And the internet? Oh, it never forgives. Entire memes are built on screenshots of *your/you're* disasters. Grammar snobs descend like vultures, correcting strangers in the comments. Half the time the correction gets more likes than the original post. People don't just notice—they celebrate your downfall.

When I'm about to type *you're,* I stop and expand it in my head. Can I swap in *you are*? If yes, it's apostrophe time. "You're amazing" = "You are amazing." Perfect. If the sentence falls apart—"I love you are dog"—then it's *your.* Simple, fast, effective.

The truth, Diary, is that this battle will never end. *Your* and *you're* are too close in sound, too easy to confuse. But that doesn't mean we shouldn't try. Because nothing undermines a heartfelt compliment, a clever argument, or a dating profile faster than the wrong form.

So the next time someone types "Your the best," I'll take a deep breath, and reply: "You're forgiven."

Yours possessively (and correctly),
The Writer Who Knows You're Going to Get It Right

Literally Too Many Words

Dear Diary,

After slogging through this parade of misused, mangled, and mistreated words, I can only conclude one thing: English is a hot mess. A glorious, chaotic, infuriating hot mess. It's like living in a house where the furniture rearranges itself every night, and somehow the sofa always ends up blocking the fridge.

We've got *literally* meaning its opposite, *irregardless* crashing the party like it belongs, *whom* clinging to life support, and *utilize* strutting around like it's important. Don't even get me started on the grocery store express lane signs. (Okay, maybe do—but only if you're prepared for the rant.)

And yet... I love it. I love that words can make us laugh when they're used badly. I love that one tiny slip—*then* instead of *than, moot* instead of *mute*—can completely change the meaning of a sentence. I love that we care enough to argue about it, even if the arguments sometimes devolve into "your/you're" slap fights in YouTube comments.

The truth, Diary, is that language evolves whether we like it or not. Today's "wrong" may be tomorrow's accepted usage. Some words will lose their sharp edges, others will be bent into new shapes, and editors like me will keep twitching every time a dictionary caves in and updates a definition. But that's the price of living with a language that refuses to sit still.

I'll keep writing my rants, catching my slips, and shaking my fist at signs in the grocery store. Because deep down, I know the battle is half the fun. English isn't a perfect system—it's a living, breathing circus. And the only thing more absurd than the words themselves is the fact that we keep trying to tame them.

But here we are. We've survived the triplets, the soap opera couples, the pretentious tuxedo-wearers, and the nausea-inducing impostors. I'm tired. I'm cranky. And I'm still in love with this ridiculous language.

Yours wordily,
The Writer Who Has Literally Run Out of Patience (and Ink)

The Ones That Got Away

Not every misused word earned a full entry in this book. Some of them are more like repeat offenders who deserve a quick mugshot before we go. Consider this the grammar police blotter—short, snappy, and just enough to make you roll your eyes.

Literally vs. Figuratively

Yes, we already tackled *literally*. But pairing it with *figuratively* deserves a note. If you say, "I literally died laughing," I'll start looking for your obituary. What you mean is *figuratively*. Unless you're a ghost writing this entry—in which case, welcome, and sorry about your untimely demise.

Impact (as a Verb)

Once upon a time, *impact* was a noun. Something collided with something else, and boom—you had an impact. Then corporate memos got hold of it, and suddenly everything is "impacting" everything else. "How will this impact our sales?" "How did the meeting impact morale?" The only thing impacted is my patience. Try *affect, influence,* or *smash into,* depending on the level of drama.

Decimate

Originally, *decimate* meant to kill one in ten. The Romans invented it as punishment for disobedient soldiers. Brutal, yes, but mathematically precise. Today, people use it to mean "completely destroy." "The hurricane decimated the town." Which technically means only ten percent of it was ruined. The other ninety percent should still be fine. Words drift, but this one drifted right off the calculator.

Peruse

This one's a sneaky trickster. *Peruse* doesn't mean "skim casually." It actually means the opposite: to read carefully, in detail. If you say you "perused the contract," I expect you to know every clause, not just that it was printed in Times New Roman. If you just glanced at it, you skimmed. You didn't peruse.

Literally Anything with Unique

Unique means one of a kind. Not "very unique." Not "kind of unique." Not "the most unique." It's like pregnancy—either you are, or you aren't. Nobody is "a little pregnant," and nothing is "a little unique." Pick a different word if you need shades of meaning. *Unusual, rare, special.* Leave *unique* alone—it's already doing the heavy lifting.

Momentarily

In American English, people use *momentarily* to mean "in a moment." "The plane will take off momentarily." Which makes me picture it lifting off for only a moment before crashing back down. The original sense is "for a moment," as in briefly. Context usually saves us, but sometimes it sounds like the captain's making very grim promises.

Hopefully

Once upon a time, *hopefully* meant "in a hopeful manner." "She looked at him hopefully." Then people started using it as a sentence adverb: "Hopefully, it won't rain." Purists still bristle, but this battle's mostly lost. Still, if you want to be crystal clear, stick with "I hope" and save yourself the side-eye.

That's All, Folks!

Well, here we are. The end of the line. This is the last official installment in the *Dear Diary Style Files,* and I'm feeling a little sentimental. (Don't worry—I won't go all "Hallmark Channel" on you. At least, not much.)

When I started this series, it was just a quirky idea: what if grammar and style guides could be funny? What if instead of stiff rules and scolding, we had diary entries, rants, confessions, and the occasional meltdown over grocery store signs? Somehow, that experiment grew into a whole collection of books, each one with its own brand of sass and snark. And you, dear reader, came along for the ride.

I've ranted about punctuation. I've squabbled with capitalization. I've dragged numbers, misused words, and formatting crimes into the spotlight. Together, we've laughed, rolled our eyes, and maybe even learned a thing or two along the way. At least, I hope so. If not, at least you got some entertainment out of my slow descent into grammar-induced madness.

So this is me signing off from the *Dear Diary Style Files.* English will keep evolving, mistakes will keep happening, and there will always be more fodder for rants. But for now, the diary is closed, the pen is capped, and I'm stepping away from the keyboard—well, let's be honest, I'll probably just start yelling at apostrophes somewhere else.

Thank you for reading, laughing, and sharing this journey with me. It's been literally unforgettable (and I mean *literally* literally).

Yours finally,
The Writer Who Actually Does Care

Also by Saoirse Temple

Bounders
The Fire of Orhowyn
The Amber Chalice

Dear Diary Style Files
Dear Diary: Punctuation Can't Save the World (But It Did Save Grandma)
Dear Diary: I Have 99 Problems and All of Them Are Numbers
Dear Diary: I Think the Alphabet is Gaslighting Me!
Dear Diary; I've Committed a Capital Offense
Dear Diary; I Don't Think That Word Means What I Think It Means

Watch for more at https://www.saoirsetemple.com/.

About the Author

Saoirse Temple is a professional editor and book coach who specializes in helping indie authors make their dream of being published come true. A long-time advocate of self-publishing, Saoirse enjoys sharing in the success of authors of all types of works. When she isn't editing or writing, she spends her time knitting, cross stitching, and exploring Grande Prairie, where she makes her home. Follow Saoirse on Facebook: www.facebook.com/saoirsetempleeditingPatreon: www.patreon.com/SaoirseTempleInstagram: @saoirsealt

Read more at www.saoirsetemple.com.

www.ingramcontent.com/pod-product-compliance
Lightning Source LLC
Chambersburg PA
CBHW031426040426
42444CB00006B/708